A Recent Revelation

Jim Rosemergy

UNITY BOOKS
Unity Village, Missouri 64065

Cover photo by L. LaMar Bell
(Mt. Rainier National Park, Washington.)

FIRST EDITION
Copyright © 1981 by Unity School of Christianity, Unity
Village, Missouri 64065. Library of Congress Card
Number 81-50146 ISBN: 0-87159-002-6.

CONTENTS

Introduction

For centuries, atheists and Christians have waged a fruitless war of words. The non-believers have fortified their positions because of the actions of the believers, and the Christians have dug deeper into the safety of creeds and dogmas because of the atheists. The battle line is as well-defined now as ever.

In spite of these differences, I believe that many Christians and atheists have something in common: few have really tried Christianity. In fact, the total spirituality that Jesus lived and taught has not been demonstrated by anyone else. Many religions have evolved; but the Truth that He presented has been exhibited by no one. Many, however, have tried to live the life and have come close!

It is my dream that this book might serve as a meeting place for both the atheist and the Christian. In this vision I see them sitting quietly, opening themselves to new possibilities.

It is the receptivity of humanity that has pushed us through the threshold of technological discoveries, and this same receptivity can be the impetus for bringing both the atheist and Christian to a greater awareness of the universe. This receptivity is fostered as scientists exhibit the courage to say no to supposed natural law. Can we who are investigating Truth itself fail to exhibit this same courage? The dogmas and creeds of traditional religion have kept us from the spirituality that Jesus taught. As did Lot's wife, we have been looking backward; thus, we have been paralyzed in our effort to move forward.

There is a way to move forward and to ascertain the mysteries of the universe. The grandest answers are given when we ask the grandest questions. This method is not new, for it is written: "Ask, and it will be given you; seek, and you will find; knock, and it will be opened to you."

For many years I felt religion was the answer to the problems plaguing the world. Although I am deeply involved in what is called religion, I now feel that religion is not the answer to the world's problems. Religion is man-made; spirituality is of God. Spirituality is the answer.

One evening during a time of despair, I asked that I might be guided into an understanding of the universal teachings of Truth that apply to all people. I asked, "What could I teach that would help to free humankind from its problems?" An angel came to me (though not the kind of being one usually thinks of when one thinks of angels; I would define my angel as a spiritual thought). It was as if a whole new area of thinking and feeling was opening for me. I wondered, as had Mary mother of Jesus, what sort of greeting this might be. A voice said that, if I wanted to be guided into a new understanding of spiritual

Truth, it would be necessary to cast aside my previous teachings and past conditionings. Nothing was to be considered sacred. My mind was to be totally open and receptive. As I responded by declaring: I am open and receptive, I could feel a wave of understanding coming.

I once looked at a darkened sky just before the rain and wind began. Though the air was still, I sensed the leading edge of the storm. That is the way I now felt. The storm that came shook my world, and the sun and the moon were darkened. For the first time in my life, I was aware of what was taking place in the book called Revelation in the Bible. In that writing there are references to earthquakes and a time when the sun and the moon cease to shine. I discovered that this occurred for me when I began to entertain new ideas; and, quite frankly, my world was shaken. Nothing seemed to be in its proper place. The sun and moon were darkened because those things that I considered most stable, such as the heavenly bodies, seemed to lose their stability.

During the months that followed I lived in the earthquake. Many of my preconceived ideas about the universe were shattered. Intuitively I knew the old ideas were not working in my life nor in the world, but it was not easy to let go of what one might call faith and stand naked before the Creator. As in any time of darkness, even the faintest light brought hope. For me, there were many times when the sun seemed to peek between the storm clouds until one day the storm passed. I cannot describe the light that now shines on me. I can only say that I now understand the teachings of Jesus and realize that they apply to all humankind. With such an understanding, the man-made barriers of religion must crumble and fall to the Earth.

For instance, I know that the only-begotten Son of God is the idea in the mind of God of what we are. This idea is manifest in the Christian, the Hindu, the Buddhist. In fact, this idea is embodied in every man, woman, and child. We are all manifestations of the only-begotten Son.

I believe that this understanding of the only-begotten Son has opened more doors to spiritual understanding than anything else I have learned. I am no longer at odds with the many religions of the world. I know that none has all the answers but that each is valid for those involved in it. There are many avenues to feeling our oneness with the Creator. It is as if the universe is a wheel. Each religion—actually each person—is a point on the edge of the wheel. The hub is God. As our awareness of our oneness with God grows, we approach the hub. At some point we notice that our brothers and sisters are walking other paths, but they are nearing the same Source upon which we have set our own eyes. Just to

Introduction

notice this commonality is to move closer to one another and, of course, closer to God.

I have learned also that Truth is always greater than we think it is. As soon as we think we have the answers, as many of the religions of the world proclaim they have, we block out the answers. God is infinite, and the truth that I speak of is an awareness of God. Thus, to say I have the truth is to say that God is finite, which cannot be true. There, although I have learned much, I am still an infant. With this discovery came the understanding of eternal life. Eternal life is not something we receive after we leave the Earth. We are immortal now. We shall never die. Eternal life is a life of continuous spiritual growth. To cease to grow in understanding is to die. Death is not oblivion; it is only a pause on our eternal journey.

The answers that I speak of came to me in a strange way. I would be moved to write from time to time, and I would usually attempt to do so. Each time that I sat to write was not a harmonious occurrence; remember the earthquake and the storm? As I began to believe the revelations I was being told, there was a tendency to consider them mine. This always broke the flow. These truths were not mine; they belonged to the universe.

Finally, I reached a point where the flow was continuous. It was what Jesus meant when He said,

" . . . whoever loses his life for my sake will find it."
*There is no conscious awareness of self. There is only
that "angel" speaking within me. Listen to the voice
that spoke within me and you will know His name;
harken to His words and you will live forever.*

Preface

The following chapters treat many of the basic points of contention between the atheist and the Christian. Each section consists of two parts. The Master's View is written as if Jesus Christ is speaking. The View of the Master's View reveals the impact the Master's View has had upon my life.

The Master's View of . . .

The Scripture

"And the gospel must first be preached to all nations."
—Mark 13:10.

For many people the Scripture is what the church is built upon; it is the soil out of which their spiritual lives seem to grow. In Truth, this is not so. In Truth, what many now call the Bible originated as a direct result of the spiritual experiences of the writers, prophets, and leaders written of in the Scripture, and of myself. The Bible did not come first; it was the product of man's encounter with the presence of God. Your Bible is like a pure spring of fresh water that emerges from a great underground stream. It is not the river but its living offspring and the evidence of the fountainhead of Truth—Spirit.

Thus, it is important for you to follow in the footsteps of those who have gone before you in spiritual growth. It is not enough to read of the beauty of God's presence; it should be your quest to experience God as the prophets and I did.

Your Bible is the blueprint that reveals the structure of your lives. The soil out of which you spring forth is Spirit, and the Bible is your guiding light. Follow it the way a flower traces the movement of the sun from east to west.

If you have eyes to see and ears to hear, you will discover the secrets of the universe. The Bible is a treasure chest of gems of wisdom and precious insights into the nature of God and humanity. If you look, you will find how the hopeless were healed and the downtrodden were lifted up; and you will find your sacred and eternal destiny.

You will discover none of these things if you solely use the powers of your intellect. Your thinking nature views life too literally. Both the believer and nonbeliever fall into this dark pit.

The nonbeliever forsakes the idea that God is a tyrant who kills men, women, and children. Intuitively, he feels God has none of these human qualities. However, because the Bible seems to reveal this vengeful God, he logically but falsely concludes that there is no God.

My friends, know this: God has none of these human qualities. The God who punishes lives only in the abyss of some minds. In Truth, the Father is like the sun shining on the just and the unjust. The early men and women felt that God would kill their enemies on their behalf. It is humanity's thought of God, not God, that is the murderer.

No matter what your understanding of the one Presence, God is always more. This is true because God is endless and infinite and cannot be totally known. The activity of Spirit has always been restricted by the channel through which it flows.

And yet, there is a message for you in these stories of the vengeful God and the conquest of the Promised Land. If you have eyes to see, you will discern that before you can enter the land of peace and fulfillment you must utterly destroy all negative beliefs and concepts that stand between you and an awareness of God. The struggles of the Old Testament are not just history; they are life. Enter into the Promised Land; but first destroy the belief that God is vengeful. Such a city is set not on a hill but in a valley.

And then there are the believers who say they believe, but who do not follow the way. Just as the nonbelievers use their intellect to deny the existence of God, so the believers use their intellect and fail to truly understand the Father. The Bible reveals the uncharted avenues of the soul. The path cannot be seen or traveled unless you shun extreme literalism and discern Truth, not events.

You have heard me say that whoever believes in me shall have abundant life. Do you not realize that I am the Way, the Truth, and the Life? It is not I as an individual but the Truth I teach that saves and frees you. You must not believe in me unless you know that I am Truth. If you were to believe in me as an individual, I would not have physically left you. But I had to leave, for my physical appearance blinded you and you could not see Truth. Having left, I can still live in you because Truth can dwell in you.

Search for the hidden manna in the Scripture and you will be fulfilled. Drink of the living water of the Scripture and you will never again thirst.

A View of the Master's View

My personal search for meaning in the Scripture has led to the discovery of the hidden manna that has transformed my life. In the past, I would read of some story or character in the Bible and it was as if I were looking through a window—I saw only what the untrained eye could see. To look through the window in this manner was to take the Bible literally. I found a literal interpretation of the Bible to be no interpretation at all. My naturally inquisitive mind became perplexed while tracing the early stories in the Bible. I was puzzled by the fact that Gen. 1:26 proclaimed the creation of man, but in Gen. 2:4 it is written that there was no man to till the soil. Upon reading the story of Adam and Eve, their son Seth had a wife when Eve was literally the only other woman on the face of the Earth. Such unanswered questions made me doubt the validity of the Scripture.

Since receiving new insight into the Scripture I no longer look through a window. Instead, I look through a prism, for I see so many beautiful colors of Truth. Before looking through the prism, I trod upon an Earth that was parched and barren; now it is a land flowing with milk and honey. The Bible has come alive now because I see it as more than a history of the Hebrew nation and the evolution of

Christianity. I see it as the history and evolution of my soul and all the souls that inhabit the universe. The Bible is a living entity because it is my story. I can look at a biblical character and see myself. In the miracles, I see patterns and spiritual principles that produce miracles in my own life.

For instance, in the feeding of the 5,000 there is a spiritual pattern that reveals the answer to the prosperity problems we must overcome. First, there is a need for nourishment. The disciples remark that it is late and that the people should be sent to the villages to buy themselves something to eat. Jesus says to His disciples, *"You give them something to eat."* The disciples balk at such an idea, and the process begins as Jesus asks, *"How many loaves have you?"*

It is apparent that the disciples see lack; but Jesus is focusing upon the food that is available. So often we are like the disciples, focusing upon what we do not have instead of what we do have. In this case it is discovered that they have five loaves and two fish. Jesus takes the food and tells the people to sit down. This is the beginning of any spiritual demonstration. We must first become still. In the stillness we focus upon our blessings rather than upon what we lack. Jesus takes the loaves and the fish and gives thanks for them. If we are to prosper, we must do likewise. If we direct our attention to what we lack, our thoughts of lack produce lack and we will lose even what we have. If we give thanks as Jesus did, our minds will be filled with thoughts of abundance and we will be given more. In the story there is an abundance left over. It is a beautiful way to portray the abundance of God's kingdom. Can you see that the feeding of the 5,000 is more than a miracle that Jesus performed? It is a pattern, which becomes a guide for practical living.

This is just one of the many gems of wisdom in the Bible. The true worth of this gem can be used to bless our lives; but first, we must have the courage to look through the prism and see the many facets of Truth that are a part of the biblical narrative. When I first discovered these things I asked, Why must it be hidden? Why are these principles not available to all? Quickly but gently the answer came. They are not hidden, but you must have eyes to see.

The Master's View of . . .

The Law of Creation

As he thinketh in his heart, so is he.
— Prov. 23:7 (A.V.).

" . . . On earth as it is in heaven."
— Mt. 6:10.

In the beginning was the Word, and
the Word was with God, and the
Word was God. He was in the beginning with God; all things were made
through him, and without him was
not anything made that was made.
— John 1:1-3.

You consider yourself to be helpless, like a leaf driven by the tireless wind. You are not compelled by the wind. It does not govern the path of your ship. Your course is determined by the use of the wind and the set of your sail. You are not a ship without a rudder. Your mind is the helm of your soul. With your mind you can set sail for the stars. Your sails are your thoughts, and they always return to their home port. Thoughts of resentment are trimmed to the winds of human conflicts, and they guide you to storms of chaotic human relationships. Thoughts of love set sail for the port of harmony and peace where all are one. The conditions of your life are not beyond your control. What you see and experience is mothered within you. War and famine are there. When there is no conflict in you or feelings of lack, war and famine vanish. When you are at peace with yourself, all people will be your brothers and sisters, and even the wolf and lamb shall lie down together. Do you not see that you are in control of your helplessness?

You create with your hands. Houses are built and fields are plowed; but remember, the mind guides your hands and is the true creator. You are not helpless; you are a creator giving form to the Father's formless creation. Although this is true, your helplessness is understandable. You are like the wind not knowing its alpha or omega. It is because you do not know the law of creation. I told you years ago, but you did not have ears to hear. Instead you have blindly used the law of creation and created chaos and confusion. You are like the child playing with the sculptor's clay—you could form a majestic statue, but most of your creations are deformed and without enduring meaning. Listen now as you hear the words once again: "On earth as it is in heaven." The Earth is your outer world, and heaven is the world of the within. The inner kingdom is ruled by each person. Your servants are obedient and do your bidding without question. These servants of the mind are the thoughts that create the earthly experience. What appears before you rests within you. Perhaps you did not even know of its arrival, but it is still a welcomed guest in your kingdom. If you loose it from within you, it will vanish from the Earth. If you choose to retain what is within you, it will abide as a part of your life experience. Still you have not thought of everything that has happened to you; but remember, your servants journey together as they create your world. As they travel, they speak with one another and, in their blind commitment to do your bidding, they distort your innermost desires. They can do this because you often have no clear view of what you seek in life. Servants make your decisions, and you do not like their judgment. Be careful of your words, for your servants are always listening. Every idle word is a command to them.

their courses. Earthquakes rumble as you tremble within. Animals are born and die, and new orders are established, as you are transmuted from the darkness of ignorance to the light of knowing. Your courage lives in the lion, and your strength expresses as the ox. Nonresistance and patience live as the tortoise, and gentleness as the lamb. Resistance in you is expressed as the stinging insect. All things were made through you.

You must assume responsibility for your creation. Do not be overcome by this commission. It is the way you have been created. You cannot escape it. Not for one moment can you flee from your creative nature. Your thoughts are your creative power. Even the distant stars feel the power of your mind. You have thought the stars determine your destiny, so you charted the movement of the heavenly bodies. When you gaze at the heavens, you are studying the kingdom of heaven lying within you. Stars do not determine your course. You guide the movement of the stars. You are the Word of God, and you use words to express what you think. The creative power is not the sound that grows faint with distant echoes, but it is the formless idea that never fades.

Do not let this insight into your role in the universe cause you to create lifeless statues of your image and golden thrones for you to sit upon. Instead, let it humble you. You are not a god; you are

the hands of God. In the past, guided by the darkness
of your ignorance, you have built crumbling civiliza-
tions and barriers to brotherhood. Now, guided by
the light of truth, our Father shall feel His hands
yield to Him, and His sacred work shall be done.

A View of the Master's View

The time has come for me to let go all excuses. I
know I will long for their company, but we must
never meet again. Their presence is no longer
needed, for nothing is standing between me and my
good except the shadow of who I thought I was. The
shadow, the helpless and inadequate one, actually
created my confusion. Of course I accused others
of being the barriers to my good, but I was the guilty
one. Problems had always resided outside of me until the Master asked me to look into the calm, reflec-
tive stillness of my soul. There I saw the same difficulties I had always seen. Is there no escape, I
thought? Spirit answered, "There seems to be no
escape, because you seek to flee from yourself.
From such a prison there is no escape." Now I know
why the Master asked me to gaze into my soul. In
the calm and stillness I would eventually discover
that the kingdom on Earth is a reflection of the kingdom within.

For years I have striven on Earth, little realizing

that the battle had to be won in heaven. *"On earth as it is in heaven"* is now my battle cry. Those six words tell me the secret of creation. They also tell me what I would like to disregard. For instance, every negative circumstance I have ever found myself a part of was a part of me. I saw such happenings as separate, but now I know there was an invisible cord linking us. By ignoring the law of creation, I found myself thrashing in the outer world of effects and becoming entangled in the cord. Knowing the law of creation enabled me to break the invisible cord and be free.

I am not of the Earth and neither are you. For eons we have been trying to establish the kingdom of heaven on Earth, when we should have been trying to live in the kingdom of heaven always available to us. *"But seek first his kingdom and his righteousness, and all these things shall be yours as well."*

This is a new way of living. It is living beyond the law of cause and effect. It is to dwell in the kingdom of God today rather than waiting for it at a later time. It will never come tomorrow if I have not found it today. Years ago I was presented with a choice. I could receive a bushel of apples or the harvested tree that would not bear fruit for another season. In my ignorance of the universe, I chose the bushel of apples and found myself starving.

Because of the Master's view, I have a new understanding. The tree is the kingdom of heaven, the
realm of causes. The bushel is the world of effects,
the kingdom on Earth. There is nothing wrong with
the bushel, for it is the fruit of the tree; but I must
know the true Source. The bushel will pass away,
but the tree will never die.

There is no need to expend large amounts of
energy on Earth. Our purpose here is a simple
one — to know God. The things of the outer world
give us pleasure, but such pleasure fades away.
Knowing God brings a joy that is full. Of course,
there are many things we need in order to exist here,
but they are the results or manifestation of what is
within us. We can seek to create an awareness of
these things within us and they will manifest in our
world, but one day they will be old and we will
discard them. Our true striving is for what does not
perish. If you have need of anything in your life,
seek to know God as the unlimited supply and your
Source, and these things will be added unto you.
This awareness will never pass away and will
become a foundation upon which even deeper
truths will build themselves. If you have a healing
need, know God as life and wholeness, and you will
be healed. Rejoice briefly in the passage of your
disease, but rejoice eternally in the truth that you
are whole. Do not strive to marry a certain person.

Instead, seek to know God as love, and the love you will become will attract to you the love you seek. Life is not to be wild imaginings and the accomplishing of many goals. There is one goal — to know God. From this one pursuit all will be fulfilled.

I am the captain of my ship, although the Master has taught me that there is One more experienced than I who helps to plot my course. I acknowledge that the winds that determine my movement are thoughts generated within my mind. It is even possible for the life I live to influence other people in some small way. Certainly I am far from helpless. The Master has taught me that, while I declare myself to be powerless, I am engaged in giving form to my world. However, the idea of the winds of my mind influencing the stars seems beyond comprehension. Still, there are the words, *all things were made through him.* Just how far does my world extend? Do the collective thoughts of all spiritual beings exert a force upon the universe? Could it be that when I tremble in fear, mountains shake? When I am at peace, the lamb and the wolf yearn to lie down together? I can believe my thoughts govern my own life. The ancients were correct—*As he thinketh in his heart, so is he*—but are there not bounds to man's thoughts? The Master would have me believe that my thoughts are heard in the far reaches of the universe, carried by His divine law of creation: *"On earth as it is in heaven."* The earth is not a planet. It is the realm of effects, manifestation wherever it occurs. Heaven is the realm of causes lying within spiritual man. I must acquiesce. Powerless, I am not. Humbled, I am. The weight of responsibility is upon me. I release the helm of my ship and seek the guidance of the One more experienced than I. The inner teacher speaks to me, "Don't concern yourself with the stars; they yield to your mind. Instead, yield to me and let the sacred work be done."

The Master's View of . . .

The Christ

For God so loved the world that he gave his only Son, that whoever believes in him should not perish but have eternal life. — John 3:16.

There was a day when I asked my disciples, "Who am I?" One of them answered, "You are the Christ, the Son of the living God." This follower caught a glimpse of my true identity; I wonder if he saw his own? Actually, he spied his own divine potential reflected in me. I wonder what he would have answered if I had asked, "And what of you, Simon Peter, who are you?" How would you answer that question? Your answer will determine who you will become.

Years before my birth prophets were proclaiming my arrival. Intuitively, they felt the coming of the Christ. The prophets felt the stirring within their souls and proclaimed a coming messiah. If their understanding could have borne it, they would have proclaimed not a man but the Christ, who took the form of a man. If they had known themselves, they would have recognized the Christ within them.

Today you are my disciples; therefore, I will ask you this question: "What is the Christ?" You might answer, "You, Jesus, are the Christ"; but your reply would be incomplete. Remember when I said, " . . . He who believes in me will also do the works that I do; and greater works than these will he do . . . "? Do you not see that I am your unfulfilled potential? I am what you are becoming. I am what you are.

All people hold within them at least a vague

image of perfection. The Jews call it the Messiah; the Christians, the Christ; the Hindus, Krishna. Whenever you dream of being more than you appear to be, you are stirring your inner God-man potential.

Every living thing unfolds according to its potential. Within the tiny mustard seed is that great shrub; within the thorny bush is the finished, unblemished rose. Within each of us is the divine pattern, which is our guide. In my time this pattern was called the Christ. Did you not know that you are the Christ? How else could you do the things that I do? That is my promise to you. Believe me and you shall become what the Father has ordained you to be.

All the illumined ones of all ages have proclaimed, "I am not special; I am only doing what you can do." Why are some made deaf by what they see? They stand in awe before me, fix their eyes upon me, and fail to hear the words I speak. Listen, for my words are Truth. You are a Son of God; you are the Christ.

A View of the Master's View

Life is a series of discoveries, and each revelation causes a stirring within the soul. Nothing has created a greater stirring in my soul than the recent revelation into the nature of the Christ. Although my soul was moved by this experience, I greeted this new illumination with doubt and a certain sense of dismay. I was troubled, for I did not want to believe what had been given. All my past training cried out when it was revealed that each of us has the potential to become the Christ. I was disturbed to discover that we are not true to what we are until we make manifest this grand idea of what we are in the mind of God. I thought my whole being would rebel at this idea, but I found only the part of me that wanted to remain in bondage was repulsed by such a declaration. Then I determined that to accept this recent revelation would not lessen what Jesus had accomplished in His life upon this planet but would be true witness of what He had taught. I was to realize that Jesus had come to teach us what we are. To grasp His teaching of the Christ was to grasp a greater understanding of my own nature.

The Way-Shower was pushing back the horizon of the spiritual frontier as He whispered in my inner ear, "You will do the works that I do and greater works than these will you do." For years I had pleaded, "Why was such a statement ever made?" Surely it could not be true; but the One who said that He was the Truth had declared it so. For years I had denied the expression of my own Christ potential by discounting that promise. I found that it was not a promise that could be denied indefinitely. I discovered that the Christ is always seeking expression in me. Every time I sought to become a better person, the inner Christ was seeking to bring that nagging promise into manifestation. It is like the seed that yearns to become a great tree. It is like the child who seeks to grow up. Within each person is the yearning to become the Christ in expression. This grand seed was planted in all hearts by the Creator.

As I began to understand the nature of the Christ, I saw new heights of human experience. Life became an inner process of giving expression to what I am. In so doing I have found an inner strength that enables me to do all things. I have discovered a limitless reservoir of unbounded love that seeks to give itself to everyone.

Jesus made this discovery about Himself and then taught that His discovery was in all people. That is why He was so loved by the multitudes. He could see something within them that they could not see within themselves. To nurture this divine seed within ourselves is to nurture it within others. It is to see that we are created equally because we are all manifestations of the same idea in the mind of God. At any given moment we are expressing the degree of our Christ potential that we choose; nevertheless, we are what we are, and we can only become what we are. To say "no" to the Christ is not to destroy but only to delay the inevitable expression of the truth of our being.

The Master's View of . . .

Prayer

"Therefore I tell you, whatever you ask in prayer, believe that you have received it, and it will be yours."
—Mark 11:24.

There is only one path to spiritual awareness. There is only one tool to build your life. I have walked this path of stillness and labored with this tool of transformation. The path and the tool have one name: they are called prayer. With this tool I have built my life. In Truth, my life is a prayer because I am always aware of the Father. He speaks to me, and always I listen. My Father is your Father. He speaks to you in a high place within you, but you do not always pause to listen. If you do pause, at first you will never want to come down from the mountain; but eventually, the voice will become so loud that you can hear it as you walk through the valley of the shadow of death.

I have not built my life with words, for prayer is not talking to God; it is experiencing the essence of Spirit. Your words are but a pathway that guides you to the secret place of the most high where you meet the Lord of your being. After you have known the Father, it will seem that you always want to return to the experience, but this is not your true desire. Instead you seek a life of prayer.

I have never sought to change my Father, for He is changeless. It is I who must change, and prayer is the sacred tool that plants the seeds of Truth which bring the change. As surely as the sun shines each day, so I experience my Father daily; thus, the seeds sprout and grow.

I have taught you how to pray and experience our Father. Promise that you will heed my words by always affirming your oneness with Him. You live and move and have your being in God. In Truth, you will never be closer to God than you are this very moment. Your quest in prayer is to know this Truth that sets you free.

As you seek to change yourself, let this be your guide: "And whatever you ask in prayer, you will receive, if you have faith."

Before you ask, remember it is written that the Father knows your needs before you speak. What then is asking? Watch a small child and you will learn the answer. As the child asks, he holds forth his hand. It is the hand, not the words, that speaks Truth. The hand reaches out to receive. It says, "I am ready." The asking is for you, not God. The asking defines the goal for you and makes a dwelling place in your mind. It prepares you to receive and to experience our Father.

And now you must believe. Only believe. You may cry out as one did years ago, "I believe; help my unbelief." As you ask to change yourself and to believe, you must affirm that what you desire now is.

If you seek peace, plant this seed: Peace; be still.

If you are blind, plant this seed: Now, I see.

If you are weak, plant this seed: The Lord is my strength. Plant such seeds and you will reap a har-

vest that has been ordained for you from the beginning.

I have watched you attempt to plant seeds with a broken tool. It was a tool I gave you; but you have broken it. I have heard you use this tool improperly many times. I grieve when I hear you say, "In the name of Jesus Christ," and I weep as I did at the grave of Lazarus. To pray in my name means to use my method of prayer. "And whatever you ask in prayer, you will receive, if you have faith." The power of prayer is not in my name, but in my way of praying.

On another day when many were gathered together on a mountain I told you to pray in a certain manner. The words you have labeled The Lord's Prayer. Always you think that prayer is words, and always you are wrong. What you call my prayer is not to be spoken but to be a guide for all prayer. When you seek to experience the Father, do so with the spiritual understanding embodied in those words rather than with the words themselves. If you understand the Truth that abides in these words, you will see the New Jerusalem. If you look for a city, you will never find it. I thought you would know it was not a place from its dimensions and because I said it would have its own source of light.

The city is what all persons seek. They seek to dwell in the house of the Lord forever. The dimen-

sions of this house make it a cube. In the temple of
the Jewish people there is such a place. It is called
the Holy of Holies; it is the dwelling place of God.
Always men have felt that the presence of God could
not be continuously experienced. I tell you the
Presence is described as a city because you can
dwell in it. The unit of construction is twelve
because it is the number of spiritual completeness.
The city or presence of God that you will experience
is adorned with jewels and gems because it is the
most precious thing of your life. All your words, your
asking, and your seeking are for the New Jerusalem.
You will know it and dwell in it when you are continuously aware of the presence of the One. That is
why I told you that I go to prepare a place for you
and that in my Father's house are many rooms.
Prayer is the path you will walk upon, and it is the
light that guides your way. True prayer is what you
seek. I wait for you in the Holy of Holies. The gates
of the New Jerusalem are never closed. Come. I wait
for you.

A View of the Master's View

As a small child I heard people speak of this
mysterious thing called prayer. I sat motionless in
church and listened as I heard the minister pray.
What else was I to assume but that prayer was

words? We even spoke words called The Lord's Prayer—words given to us by the Master of prayer, Jesus. This only seemed to reinforce the idea that prayer was words. From such misconceptions came the idea that God must be listening; therefore, my words must be loud (possibly God is hard of hearing), and at the very least the words had to be eloquent.

When problems began to arise prayer was declared to be the answer. Pray about them, I was told. Then the real problem occurred. I prayed but nothing happened. The learned ones declared, "God has answered and His answer is no." I retorted, "But I prayed for healing. Doesn't God want all people to be healed?" "It was God's will," I was told. From such experiences I began to dislike God and the sacred tool called prayer. Soon I considered prayer a tool to be used only by the clergy and other religious people. For a time I turned my back upon God and prayer, but soon I was responding to the movement of Spirit within me; I was once again searching for guidance concerning prayer. Undoubtedly, the answer came in a moment of prayer, and I did not even realize it.

The realization came that prayer is not words. The words were simply vehicles that brought me to prayer. This understanding did not come all at once. First came the idea that prayer was listening to God.

How often I sat in silence wishing for a loud, boom-
ing voice that would call out to me! Next I thought
that prayer was communion between God and myself. This idea was comfortable until I realized that
God is omnipresent and therefore dwells within me.
To speak of God *and* me would be to declare a
separation between us.

One evening I opened the Bible and read the
words, *In the beginning God . . . ,* and I stopped.
There was the answer. There is only God. True
prayer is knowing that there is only God and experiencing His presence and power. Once I had this
experience I vowed to seek it continuously. I sought
to dwell within it. It is what Jesus called the New
Jerusalem. It is not a physical city but a state of
being, in which I am to become aware of the presence of God every moment of my life. It is the goal
of everyone who inhabits the Earth. We call it by
many names, but it is the only goal. The paradox is
that we continuously dwell in this precious city. We
are as close to God this very moment as we will ever
be. The quest is to become aware of this Truth; and
prayer is the answer.

Begin by trying to relax. Declare that you are
relaxed, and relaxation will be yours. Say to yourself: *I am relaxed and at peace.* Speak these words
slowly and often until you feel yourself relaxing;
then let go and become at peace. In this relaxed

state declare that you are one with the only presence and the only power, and it will be yours. Say to yourself: *I and the Father are one.* Speak the words slowly and often until they fill your mind. Then begin to contemplate the statement. Ask what it means and listen for new insight. Open yourself totally to the coming experience. Open your mind and your feeling nature and allow Spirit to pick the channel. If your mind begins to drift, declare: *I and the Father are one.* In time you will experience the oneness of true prayer as you discover that there is only God. This is only the beginning, for you will experience the presence and power in many ways. You will live not in a city of gold but in the preciousness that only comes by feeling the presence of God.

The Master's View of . . .

Practicing the Presence of God

Enoch walked with God . . . —Gen.
5:24.

'In him we live and move and have
our being.' —Acts 17:28.

Pray constantly . . . —I Thess. 5:17.

In the beginning, God . . . . *In such a truth lies the genesis of your life. You shall capture the essence of those words as you traverse the courtyard of a fallen temple. Before you are broken tiles, shattered columns, and breathless, lifeless idols. All that remains is a lone wall inscribed with the words:* There is only God. *The rubble of the temple makes a silent statement and pleads to know the answer to a simple question, "We believed in our God; how did this befall us?"*

Is this not a question you have asked as you surveyed the ruins of your life? If you had been present the day the ground shook, you might have noticed the inscriptions etched upon opposing walls of the temple. Ours Is The Only Way *was imprinted upon one wall, and inscribed on the other were the words:* There Is Only God. *No temple can stand with a truth upon one wall and a lie written on the other. Yet, another temple is to rise in the place of the fallen one.* There Is Only God *is to be its cornerstone. Four walls will rise which restrict no man. The new temple is your daily life.*

A new vision awaits you. It is the promised land flowing with milk and honey. You need not travel to a distant country to experience the joy of this kingdom. The ground upon which you stand is sacred soil. You live and move and have your being in God. It is your mission in life to feel and experience this presence and power. To do so is to join Enoch in a walk with God. It is to join the Apostle Paul in praying without ceasing and to call our Father "friend," as did the patriarch Abraham. You walk into this relationship with a timeless and enduring truth constantly passing your lips — There Is Only God. I behold the Father in all things.

From this moment life becomes your teacher. You raise your eyes to the sky and witness the great bird lifted by the unseen presence and power of the wind. You admire the bird's lofty perch and the view of the kingdom he must have. You salute his trusting spirit and ability to rest easily in the everlasting arms of the wind. As you stand searching the sky for other birds, you spy the remaining wall of the temple and its sacred inscription: There Is Only God. Suddenly you feel the uplifting, unseen presence and power of the Father. You sense your grip loosening on your life and a relinquishing of your will. You too have been lifted up, and you behold a new world and experience a new pinnacle of living. The new temple has begun its rise from ruin.

All nature now becomes the Father's messenger of life. The trees dancing with the gentle caress of the wind cause you to sway with joy as the invisible Spirit of God is moving through the uppermost branches of your mind. Life has now taken on new meaning. It is a searching for our Father in all things.

Go to the shores of your lands and stand feebly in the raging surf. You can feel water running between your legs and your feet sinking into the sand, or you can feel the relentless power of God and the solid foundation that such a knowing forms beneath you. Can you not see that God is present in all things? Our senses are now attuned to His presence and power. We practice the presence of God until our lives are housed in the golden splendor of the New Jerusalem. Did I not tell you the New Jerusalem was a continuous awareness of the Father's presence? What could be more precious than such a temple? Even gold is reduced in its brilliance and value when compared to the peace and joy Spirit is. Practice the presence of God until the walls of the temple stand erect and your life is a prayer.

Sleep in His peace, wake in His joy, walk in His light, and be warmed by His love. Rise with the sun and let your first thought be not the things you must do that day but the delightful task of feeling the presence enfolding you. Let the first physical movement you make be accomplished with the acknowledgment of the strength and life of our Father that make all activity possible. These thoughts will make the simplest movement an act of worship. Now even the breaking of bread throughout the day is done in remembrance of the feeding of the 5,000 and the unlimited supply that can nourish all mankind. As you are nourished by your daily bread, you know you must daily partake of Truth if you are to grow in stature in the kingdom of God. As you speak, give thanks for the power of the Word by echoing words you first hear uttered by the Spirit of Truth within you. Prepare yourself, for the words you hear will be unifying, harmonizing, and loving. Let these words extend into your relationships with people. Within every person you meet lies the presence of God in silent repose. This spark of Spirit within each individual quickens the struggle that gives birth to the divine flame. Fan this spark of Spirit until it is ablaze as light and love. Silently salute the divinity in each person you meet, and the divine Spirit will begin its rise into expression. For every unexpected good, give thanks to the Father. You have but one Source, and life grows in richness when you praise the unseen, unlimited supply God is. Do not shudder in fear and doubt when you face a challenging task. Do you not realize that you are not alone? If you cannot sense the presence of power within you, at least behold God in the midst of your challenge. Hidden in each difficulty is an opportunity to walk with God. Where there appears to be death, there is life. Where there appears to be sickness, wholeness is the attending physician. Where there appears to be lack, a window to heaven has opened. God is in the midst of all things. There Is Only God.

Do you often feel an uneasiness during your day, an aloneness that even a human friend or a crowd cannot fulfill? Such feelings are a call to listen to the Spirit of Truth and to speak the words you hear echoing within. Always the message is the same, "You and I are one." Gently whisper what you hear, and your uneasiness and aloneness will disappear into the nothingness from which they came.

It is good to be still. Likewise, it is good to feel the stillness of the Father's presence and power in all activity. It is practicing the presence of God. As you walk with your Friend, God, and pray without ceasing, mountains may rise in your path, but they will be leveled by the awareness of His power. From these crumbling mountains stone masons will carry rocks that will become the walls of a new temple you are building with your daily life.

A View of the Master's View

When I stood in the courtyard of rubble and observed the lone wall of the temple declaring *There Is Only God,* I did not understand why it alone survived the earthquake. Now I have a better understanding. The Master's view has helped me. Still, I do not fully comprehend the depth of those words, but they have become my friends, and like all friends, they help me to be who I am.

My friends have initiated the life I now attempt to live. My unfolding spiritual life is no different from yours. In the beginning, I grew spiritually in spite of my prayer life rather than because of it. Prayer was not the inner knowing that there is only God. Instead it was bent knee and beseeching voice compelled by a seeming tragedy. This tainted understanding of prayer gave rise to a negative response when prayer was mentioned. My mind would ask, "Has it gotten so bad we have to pray about it?" Since tragedies were not a common occurrence in my life, neither was prayer. Next followed the sporadic nightly vigil of telling God my problems. Of course, not only did I outline the difficulties, I also suggested solutions I would find acceptable. This soliloquy frustrated me, for the problems remained. It seemed God either did not hear my eloquent King James rhetoric or, if He did hear my words (and could understand them), He did not care. I suppose sometimes an answer was revealed, but since it was not the exact outcome I had recommended, I was not aware of the good unfolding in my life. Today I realize I was not building a temple of daily prayer. I was not even going into the closet as the Master had recommended. At this time in my life, I could have stood in the courtyard of the fallen temple and not seen the wall containing the inscription: *There Is Only God.* Instead I would have looked at the ruins of my life, knelt in the sand, and etched the falsehood: *there is no God.*

Still, Spirit was active within me (a place I never dreamed to look), and before I wiped the sand from my hands, I learned of affirmative prayer. It was a proclamation of Truth. *God is healing me now,* I declared, and wholeness sprang forth within my soul and body. I affirmed: *God is providing for my every need.* The needs were fulfilled, and I began to believe God really cared. He was not as far away as He had once seemed. In fact, there were times I felt I could feel His presence and power within me. Prayer became not a heap of words but a heightened adventure. Finally, I had found the inner place where the temple was to be built.

In this temple, prayer was not just a tool to live life more fully, but a life fully lived. Prayer, which had begun as a desperate cry for help, was now the life I sought to live. I knew that in the past I had not really sought healing; I had sought the prayerful experience of wholeness. I had not sought prosperity in tangible form; I had chased an awareness of the Source that supplies every need. These fleeting glimpses of the kingdom of God gave birth to a diligent effort to sit in silence each day. One day while struggling with the silence, the words *There Is Only God* drifted effortlessly into my mind. The words became etched on my heart, and the genesis of my life occurred.

These words are more than an inscription written on the wall of the temple; they are its cornerstone. From this rock rises a life keenly and perpetually aware of the Father's presence and power. How could such a temple be built? How could such a life be lived? Does it mean a retreat into a world of prayer? For many, such a journey would be not into a world of prayer but away from a world of problems and people. Such a pilgrimage would circle the Earth and return once again to the courtyard of the fallen temple.

Jesus took no such journey. He did not live in a cave. He stood in the light and beheld God in all things. He did this because He knew *There Is Only God*. The Master beckons to each of us to search the sky, stand in the raging surf, and build a temple no earthquake can reduce to rubble.

I have searched the sky and have seen only the bird. At other times I have felt myself lifted to its heights of perception. I have stood feebly in the surf and felt only water and sand, but at other times I have become one with the rhythm and power that run deeper than the sea. I have delighted in the fragrance of the rose, but I have also seen and heard its message. The rose has whispered to me, "I am a thing of beauty, but I am adorned with thorns. Learn from me. Beauty is to be experienced. You are not to touch it; it is to touch you. Beauty withers when you hold it, but it grows when you let it hold you."

To be lifted by the thought of the bird, to stand in the ocean and feel more than water and sand, and to be taught by the rose is to practice the presence of God. To behold God in these things and all life is our destiny. It points to the message on the lone wall of the temple. Have you not felt waves of peace and joy when there was seemingly no reason to be peaceful or joyful? I once believed peace and joy needed an outer cause. It is not true. They "pass understanding," for their cause is not of this world. The outer world gives and takes away. In the inner kingdom peace flows from the stillness of Spirit, and joy bubbles from the lake of love. They cannot pass away; they must pass through us. If we seek a reason to be peaceful or joyful, these gifts of God will slip through our fingers as the water we hold to our lips when we thirst. If we seek only peace and joy, we will never thirst again.

I have felt the love and blessing of other people. They lifted me, but their words and acts of praise seemed to die as the echo of the wind. Too often I have yearned for this love while others around me have longed for someone to bless and love them. While building my temple of daily prayer, I discovered that perpetually blessing others kept me in a continuous awareness of the Father's love. Prac-

ticing the presence of God in this way has led to an
abiding understanding of the law, "Nothing is yours
until you give it away."

The temple is rising. The rocks from the mountains are being lifted into place. With the temple
comes a new perception and a joyful, playful absurdity to life.

One day I was sitting and watching the wind
move the uppermost branches of several large oak
trees. Suddenly a laughing voice spoke within me:
"It is not the wind that moves the branches of the
tree; the tree moves and causes the wind."

"What?" I exclaimed. "That is ridiculous." It was
ridiculous when I first heard it and it still is today,
but such absurdity of thought assures me of new insights into life. Do you understand? If you cannot
consider what you think is absurd, how will you
ponder what you cannot fully comprehend?

As the temple rises, I stand upon the wall and
relentlessly search for the good. It is a striving to
behold God in all things. Physical movement exists
so I might feel the power God is. Decisions are to be
made so I might know more fully the infinite wisdom God is.

There is a merging with life, a reverence for life, a
fascination with life's smallest expressions. One day
another absurdity occurred. Two small expressions
of life, a caterpillar and I, met on the road of life.

Perhaps we were both practicing the presence that day. We sensed one another's presence. I saw him, and I could see him searching for me. He knows I am, and I know he is. We have touched. In the knowing faculty within each of us rests the mind of God. We each move and give testimony that we are linked in the life God is.

At times there is a giddiness and a joyful laughter when there is nothing to laugh about. Why, I don't know. Perhaps it is the divine fountain of joy surfacing for a time in my soul. At other times, the stream of joy cascades down my face as tears. I don't know why. Would that I was open to the hidden fountain more often!

There is more that has been and more that shall be. The temple is rising, but its cornerstone assures me of still higher walls, walls that reach into the infinity of God. You have your temple of continuous prayer to build. I have mine. Together let us bless one another, pray constantly, walk with God, and call Him Friend.

The Master's View of . . .

The Sacraments

"Take, eat; this is my body . . . Drink of it, all of you; for this is my blood of the covenant, which is poured out for many for the forgiveness of sins." — Mt. 26:26-28.

"Receive the Holy Spirit." — John 20:22.

Long ago, the prophets sought to shatter the idols that man had constructed to worship. These men of God knew there could be no substitutes for Truth. They knew that symbols were a part of man's spiritual life but that a symbol's value is only in what it represents. If symbols are to have any impact upon your life, they must point to God and Truth. When you fail to look beyond a symbol, it becomes an idol. It is like trying to drink from an empty cup when you are expecting living water. Your thirst only grows.

If the prophets were to walk the Earth today, their quest would still be to destroy the idols that are worshipped in the streets and on the altars of the temples and the churches. Your puzzled reply might be, "But we know nothing of these idols you speak of." This is because your vision does not extend beyond the idol; therefore, you know nothing of the truth behind the symbols you have been given.

If I asked you these questions, what would be your reply? Can you be baptized without water? Can you partake of the Lord's Supper without the bread and the wine? You can, only if you understand the water, the bread, and the wine to be symbols, not idols. You can, if your vision extends beyond the limited horizon of the symbols. If you see a symbol's purpose, you have no real need of that symbol. It becomes only a familiar guide and friend, not to worship, but simply to remind you of the essence of life.

If the River Jordan were to cease flowing, John the Baptist would stand in the dry river bed and still baptize as he did many years ago. John knew that water cleanses only the body and that it is the mind and heart that truly must be cleansed. The water is a friendly reminder of a spiritual process in which one is cleansed of all negative thoughts and feelings. You may receive baptism by John, for to do so is to rid your soul of all that is impure; but you must also receive my baptism.

My baptism is of the Holy Spirit. What can I tell you of this Holy One? If the air you breathe is God, then the Holy Spirit is the wind. It is the movement of God through you into expression. I gave my disciples the key to this baptism when I said to them, "Receive the Holy Spirit." I foresaw after my death and resurrection a time when these frightened men would turn not to me, but to the Spirit within them. At that moment they would be receptive to my Father. The infilling would kindle a faith so strong that many would say that fire was dancing upon them. Their infilling came on the Pentecost; yours can begin today. Be receptive, as the little child.

I wish you could have been with my disciples and me in the Upper Room. I wish you could have felt the love and friendship there. I knew it was to be our last time together before the trials were to begin. We shared a meal that would nourish us forever. You have celebrated the supper many times, but many times you have left the table still hungry. It has been as I have said: You have taken the cup to your lips expecting living water and have found the cup to be empty.

I ask you now to come with me to the Upper Room and sit and share the Last Supper. If you seek a room in the city, you will not find me, because the Upper Room is found within your soul. It is a place of communion with the Father in which you will find enlightenment. You will take the bread in your hands and eat of it and discover such nourishment that you will never hunger again. You will press the cup to your lips and be nourished by living water. You will never thirst again. Since the Upper Room is within your mind, it is in this sacred place that you must uncover the meaning of the bread and the blood.

On one occasion, I told my disciples to beware of the bread of the Pharisees. They amused me when they searched for bread they could hold in their hands; but soon they found I was speaking of the teachings of the religious leaders of our day. Their teachings were not Truth and could give no true nourishment. The bread I offer my disciples and you is my teachings, which are Truth. When you partake of Truth, it brings you nourishment of which you have never dreamed. It is the hidden manna that only the Father can give. When I spoke of blood, many

*did not understand. They were thinking of the law,
which forbids the drinking of blood. Do you not
know that I was speaking of life? What is Truth if it is
not lived? What is the sun if it does not have an Earth
to shine upon? You must drink my blood, for you
must live the Truth I gave you. Drink my blood, and
you will live a life that even the saints see only as a
vision. The physical food and drink you partake of
build your body; so the blood I offer you will build
your life. Only you can eat and drink what I have
offered. That is why I spoke of eating and drinking so
often in my ministry. Who can eat food or drink for
you? And how often do you do so? You eat and drink
each day; so you must live Truth each day.*

*Come; a place has been prepared for you at my
table. Journey to the Upper Room and sup with me.
We shall share a meal that will nourish us forever.*

A View of the Master's View

Now, do you feel the message of the sacraments
as I do? These mysterious rituals have always
intrigued me, yet they seemed to withhold their
treasure from me. It is now evident that I thought
that the symbols were the treasure. I was wrong.
How many times did I partake of the Lord's Supper
but did not understand the meaning of that sacra-
ment? It is as He has said: I was expecting food and

living water; thus I returned to my seat empty. My
first response was to wonder what was wrong with
me. The other people appeared so satisfied. One
day I had the courage to speak of my emptiness,
and it became evident that I was not alone. We ate
and drank the symbols but failed to realize that
they were only symbols. Not to understand what the
bread and the wine signified is like peering into a
bottomless pit—the light is swallowed up in darkness.

But now there is a sacredness to the Lord's Supper
that touches me. It is not just a celebration that
finds its origin in the distant past in a hidden room;
it is a celebration of life. I know that the sacred process of appropriating the Truth and living the Truth
in my life is to be entered into not once a month but
once a moment. Hopefully, I can now participate in
the Last Supper as I am about my work. I can sit
alone upon a hill and sup with the Lord of my being
and eat the bread. Then I can rise and enter into life
drinking the blood and eating the bread as I live the
Truth I have been given.

I have also been puzzled by the meaning of baptism. Maybe it began years ago when I was held in
the arms of a smiling gentleman as he sprinkled
water upon me. Perhaps I wondered what manner of
circumstance this might be. Of course, I do not
remember the baptism I had as a child; but I do

remember the baptism that occurred later in life.
While I was still young, my parents told me of my infant christening, but it held no real meaning for me.
As I grew older, I was amused by the smiles and
tears upon the faces of the adults in a church ser-
vice when a child would be baptized. Always the
question formed in my mind: how could this beautiful child need to be cleansed of sin? He hasn't even
had the opportunity to make the mistakes I have
made. I wondered if it wouldn't be better for the
minister to wait until the children become adults
and then to baptize them. A problem resulted when
I became an adult and still did not understand baptism. I noticed that the church used water but that
Jesus did not. Why then was there an insistence
upon the use of water? Can you see my dilemma?
The standard ideas that surrounded baptism in
shrouds of mist left me empty once again. There has
to be more, I thought. I could understand the impor-
tance of John's baptism and its cleansing; but to me
that seemed to be a continuous process.

It is true that you will find if you seek. The Christ
Spirit spoke within me, and I discovered that the
baptism is an infilling. I also learned that this movement of the Holy Spirit depended upon me. That is
why Jesus' words are so important. Remember that
when He baptized His disciples He enjoined them,
"Receive the Holy Spirit." Therein lies the key. It is

receptivity. We must receive the activity of God into our lives. When we are receptive and open, the infilling will begin. It is like going to answer the door to allow a friend to enter. In this case, the friend is the movement of God into your life. How many times have you not even cracked the door when Spirit knocked? However, the knocking continues; and when you are open, the blessed experience begins. It is the ability to be receptive and to accept the gift of God that determines the divine flow in our lives. Perhaps the baptism is performed when we are infants because when it occurs we are just beginning life. But every day of my life is now a beginning, for every day I take time to open myself to the Holy Spirit. That simply means that I am receptive to the movement of God into my life. It is as if I can hear the knock at the door, *"Receive the Holy Spirit."*

The Master's View of . . .

The Sabbath

"Remember the sabbath day, to keep it holy. Six days you shall labor, and do all your work; but the seventh day is a sabbath to the Lord your God." — Exodus 20:8-10.

You have made a ritual of something that does not exist. The Sabbath is not a day. In Spirit, there is no time. There is only the eternal now. As you dwell upon the Earth, the eternal now is as close as you will venture into a realization of eternity. Yet, the Sabbath is a part of eternity, for it is a part of the creative process. To teach you that the Sabbath is a phase of the creative process, I healed persons on what you understood to be the Sabbath.

If you look beyond your rituals, you will remember the Sabbath and keep it holy. To fulfill this commandment, you must know the spiritual meaning of the Sabbath. It is a state of mind in which you rest from your activity and allow the Father to work. Lift up your eyes as I have, and you will see the Sabbath in the soaring eagle. The eagle climbs until he feels himself gently lifted by the winds, and then he rests and allows that unseen force to carry him. The eagle knows the meaning of the Sabbath, but you do not. As a child, you knew the Sabbath and how to keep it holy. It is only as you matured that you experienced it as a day and thus did not experience it at all. As a child, you released a seed and allowed it to rest within the earth. You tenderly covered it with moist soil and waited for the first blade to tell you of new growth. The wisdom of the child is like that of a saint, for the little one does not uncover the seed each day to see if it is growing. Instead, he waits in anticipation for the evidence of the activity of life. The Sabbath is that time in which you rest and wait for the new life.

Can you not see that the Father did the same thing on the "seventh day"? You will see that this is so when you understand the creation story. Have you not found it strange that after it is written, "Let us make man in our image, after our likeness," you can find these words, . . . and there was no man to till the ground? How could man be created and not be present to till the earth? It is because the creation story you know so well was first formed in the mind of God. The man first revealed lived not upon the Earth but as an idea in the mind of God. The first seven "days" did not rise and set with the sun. Likewise, they were ideas in the mind of God. All things begin this way. First, there is involution and then evolution. The initial creation is the creation of the creative process. It was only after the "seventh day," or the Sabbath, that . . . the Lord God formed man of dust from the ground. With those words, Adam took his first breath. And so the Sabbath is the last stage of any creative act. For you and me, it is a state of mind in which we rest from our activity and allow the activity of Spirit to move through us. When you know this, you too will say, "My Father is working still, and I am working."

I have watched so many of you pray, yet your

prayers are never answered because you will not enter into the Sabbath. To honor the Sabbath, you must let go and let the Father's work be done. You did it as children when you planted the seed. Will you do it now? If you seek healing, pray, rest from doubt, and allow the healing activity of life to move within you. If you seek prosperity, pray, rest from worry, and allow the abundance of the universe to enter into your life. You will know the Sabbath because there is a great stillness there. A peace that passes understanding will sweep over you. Imagine the stillness and the peace that existed in the mind of God just before you were formed from the dust of the ground. As you took your first breath, you took your place in the creative process as the Word of God.

A View of the Master's View

Did you know that anything that is truly spiritual must apply to all people? Many people sense this truth moving within them, and therefore find difficulty with the idea of the Sabbath. It appears not to be the same for all. Some celebrate the "day" of rest on Saturday; some, on Sunday. How could this be if that which is truly spiritual must be the same for all? Does this mean that the Sabbath is not a spiritual activity even though intuitively we know that the Sabbath is a holy event? Let me tell you how I discovered the Sabbath.

One of the most beautiful things that has happened to me was assuming responsibility for my own life. That blessed event occurred when I realized that it was thought which ruled my life and that no one can think for me. At first this realization was rather distasteful because of all the negative conditions I had brought into my life; but that soon changed. I began to look for the good circumstances in life and to realize that through the power of thought I could change any condition I was not enjoying.

As I pondered how I might change a particular event in my life, I asked how I was to begin with this momentous task. The answer was so simple that at first I laughed at it. My guidance said to become still. Become still, I thought. What kind of directive is that? I did not follow my guidance, but as time passed I began to see the validity of such a beginning. I noticed that when Jesus was about to feed the 5,000, He asked them to sit down—in other words, to get still. On other occasions people were told to close the door. All these simple occurrences provided guidance into the realm of creation. After we are relaxed, the real work commences as we begin to think thoughts that build an awareness of whatever it is that we seek in our lives. If it is healing we need, then we fill our minds with thoughts of wholeness. If it is prosperity we seek, then we think abundance and give thanks for the blessings that we do have. Though the human needs are endless, the process is the same.

It was startling to me when I found that the last step in the creative process was the same as the first—to become still. This is where the Sabbath touches the life of every spiritual being in the universe. This is where the Sabbath becomes the missing link between an idea and the manifestation of that idea. The Sabbath is a state in which we rest and allow God to move into our lives. It is a time when our work is done, and the best we can do is allow Spirit to do its work. When we understand this simple yet profound truth, we become free of worry, filled with faith, and aware that the Sabbath is not a day. It is a state of mind.

The Master's View of . . .

Good, Evil, and Sin

" . . . You will know the truth, and the truth will make you free." — John 8:32.

"Blessed are the pure in heart, for they shall see God." —Mt. 5:8.

Long ago our Father revealed to me the garden of my soul. In the midst of the garden He sowed the seed of the tree of life and admired its fruit called Truth. Nearby He planted the tree of the knowledge of good and evil. It was a stunning tree with both Truth and error beckoning from its branches. Error hung upon the outer limbs reaching out to me, while Truth grew deep within the foliage of the tree. Although shaded from the sun, the Truth shone with its own light. The Father told me He hoped this second tree would wither and die within me.

I asked, "Why establish a seedling you hope will perish?"

He answered, "Truth is to be your daily bread, but you may choose to starve."

Then I understood the garden of my soul. My food is Truth, and when I eat of it I behold only good. Only Truth can nourish me, but I am free to choose to believe what is not true. Such a choice would result in error, and the child of error is not called good; he is christened evil.

Looking at the garden of my soul, I see the tree of the knowledge of good and evil. It promises me life and power, but its gifts are sin and death. This rootless one will never stand erect in the soil of my mind, for I do not believe what is not true. Its leaves are curled and its bark is peeling, for I have never nourished it with the power of my belief.

Examine the garden of your soul and you will find these two trees. For many of you, the tree of life and its fruit remain untouched, while the outer limbs of the tree of the knowledge of good and evil are bare. You have turned your backs upon Truth, embraced error, and thus chosen to starve. The grass beneath the tree of the knowledge of good and evil has been trampled as you stand daily and harvest its unwholesome fruit by believing what is not true. Even the path to the tree of life has not been trod upon. You have been like the Earth turning from the light and experiencing night. For those who eat of the tree of life, there is no night. They stand in the noonday sun casting no shadows and echoing the pronouncement of our Father— it is good.

Don't you see now? Our Father created the tree of the knowledge of good and evil, but its seed was conceived because you were created free. A child of possibilities are you, a maker of choices. Half asleep are you, yet yearning to awake. Let these words awaken you, "Blessed are the pure in heart, for they shall see God." Your vision has been obscured by what you believe. Do you believe you see the world through your eyes? It is not so. Your mind is the lamp of your body. It is your eye. With it the world is varying shades of good and evil. Shadows in the night create fear. Shadows of the mind create evil. But your mind is more than an eyeglass. It is the creator of your life experiences.

When you pronounce a happening to be evil, look within yourself. The foggy mist of error has clouded your vision. Your heart is impure and you cannot see what God has created. You see only the fleeting creation of man. There is another way. Purify your heart, and you will see the same world your Father beheld on the seventh day. You too will rest in the goodness of the creation.

Look about you now. You have proclaimed much to be evil. Seek such events and you may spy the straggler persistently in pursuit bearing his gift of goodness. In your searching for evil events, recall my Crucifixion. Many spoke of the error and evil of Pilate and the priest. If those who spoke had withheld their pronouncement just three days, what would they have proclaimed? Surely they would have spied the straggler and his gift of goodness, for the Resurrection was made possible by Pilate and the priest. Now search for evil events in your life. Wait three days before you make your judgment. On the first day, let your gaze fall upon the ground around you, and you will find the debris of the fruit of the tree of the knowledge of good and evil. Reach down and gather this refuse into your hands and examine it. In your hands are the errors you have thought to be true. Let them speak to you once again. Perhaps they will say to you, "Life is a struggle and you must suffer." Do not believe it. They may say to you in an alluring voice, "You can obtain your good at the expense of another person." Do not believe it. Listen carefully, for the error you have believed to be true will be revealed.

On the second day release this refuse and vow never to believe its message of misery again. Before you turn to walk away, say to it, "Life need not be a struggle. There is no virtue in suffering." Pause and speak again, "In my Father's house there is enough for all. His supply is unlimited, and each receives according to the size of his cup." Let the words given to you flow easily from your heart as it is made ready to receive what is true.

On the third day make your way to the tree of life. Eagerly reach up and take the fruit called Truth. Eat of your daily bread, and what you need to know will be revealed to you. Lift your eyes and behold the world created for you from the beginning.

You have been created free. Your freedom is so great that you can choose to starve and to live in bondage. But when you choose freedom, you are free indeed. To believe what is not true is your only sin. It bears the child you have christened evil. You feel you must nourish the child, but this misconception of your mind must perish. This child has thrown mud upon your eyes and repeatedly led you to the tree of the knowledge of good and evil. The cre-

*ation of your mind has turned upon you and caused
you pain and death. Still, you can learn from this
false leader. He reveals to you what you must never
believe again. This is his gift to you.*

*Each challenging happening in your life carries
with it an even greater gift. If you only have eyes for
the so-called evil condition, you will fail to see the
straggler that persistently follows in pursuit. It is the
greater gift of the Truth that sets you free.*

A View of the Master's View

Questions, the folly and the genius of the mind!
They grow out of frustration, and their answers
often baffle us even more. Yet, it is not the answers
we seek but Truth, the divine accuracy enabling us
to see the eternal good and experience the peace
that passes understanding. I am told of the eternal
good and the goodness of creation, but what of the
evil conditions that abound on our planet? This
paradox asks its inevitable question: "Why does
there have to be evil? Who creates these
conditions?" I actually asked *myself* these questions, but I did not feel capable of an answer; so I
turned to those more "learned" than I. Their
answers came from the dead past: "Satan is the orig-
inator of evil, and he wages a fruitless battle against
God's forces of good."

"Fruitless!" I exclaimed. "It appears the evil one is winning."

Another static answer, "Yes, it appears he is; but God will prevail and evil will cease."

Their answers calmed the frustration of my soul for a time, but the genius of mind formed another puzzler: "Why does God allow such evil? Is it possible that God cannot prevent evil and is doomed to an eternal battle?" For these questions there was no answer from the past, and no one could reply in the present.

I had received answers, but they were the same unsatisfactory replies you have heard when you have made the same inquiries. The search for Truth continued. I knew my soul would know when it heard Truth. Finally it turned, not to ones more "learned," but to the Christ child inside me. Actually the Christ Spirit is not a child, but our relationship was in its infancy. I asked about the cause of evil. I was told to look about me and find the evil one. I found no devil or personification of evil, but at the scene of every crime and atrocity stood at least one person. I concluded that humans must be involved in the creation of the evil conditions of our planet.

In turning to the Christ, I asked again: "Why does God allow such evil? Can't He prevent its formation?" The answer explained the origin of the tree of the knowledge of good and evil: "If man is created free to know Truth, he must also be free to know error."

"Why doesn't God destroy the war, the crime, and the famine? Surely an all-powerful God can stop such happenings." Slowly the Spirit of Truth replied, "God does not destroy. He is not at war. God is a creator and He creates only good. For God to destroy would mean all-knowing intelligence had made a mistake. Surely no one could believe such a miscalculation is possible. It is man who is at war. He is in conflict with his own creation."

These words and the Master's view have rocked me, but from the rubble of the earthquake has come understanding. The Bible taught me the first sin was eating of the tree of the knowledge of good and evil. It was the Master who stated it was the only sin. It is believing what is not true. This belief has power in its effects. I see evil because I believe what is not true. I nourish so-called evil conditions by allowing my mind to grasp error. God knows no evil. God is Truth, and in Truth there is no error; without error evil is impossible. Remember, God pronounced His creation good. It could have been no other way. Man, being made in the image and after the likeness of the Father, has the same power of proclamation. Man names a thing and determines its nature in his own eyes. Different men will see different things.

Those who know Truth will see good. Those who believe error will perceive evil.

Such an understanding makes me dream a new dream. It brings new meaning to the Master's words, " . . . *You will know the truth and the truth will make you free."* *"Blessed are the pure in heart, for they shall see God."* To purify the heart is to find a place for Truth within the soul. There Truth will abide and be at home. From within the heart of man, Truth will behold the Resurrection while Jesus the Christ still hangs on the Cross. It will look within any condition and see Truth waiting to be recognized.

What a world this is! At times I see the creation the Father proclaimed. There are days I see God expressing Himself as the woman behind the counter at the corner store. He is the new beginning rising out of a near-fatal accident. God even teaches patience to the angry motorist leaning upon his horn. Even in the wounded soul of the person who has experienced the death of a loved one, there is good. Standing nearby is the eternal life, the departed one wishing the one in anguish could hear him say, "There is no death."

There is no evil. There are only dim forms we mistake for reality when we believe what is not true. If I can only know the truth of any situation, I will see the distorted and twisted form of evil transformed into good. Such ideas are best embraced while at peace, but principles of Truth remain whether we stand in the light or crouch in the shadows. Because of one sin I have created a distorted world existing only in my mind. Now there is another kingdom flickering across my inner vision. I do not seek fleeting glances of this world of good; I desire to dwell there.

The Master's View of . . .

Death

"O death, where is thy victory?
O death, where is thy sting?"
—I Corinthians 15:55.

You have watched the sunrise and said that it marks the birth of day. You have seen the sun sink behind the mountains and thought that the day had died. You were wrong, for the rising sun bears the day, and the setting sun the night. Neither dies; both are born. When the sun rises upon a person, you call it birth; and when it sets, you call it death. You are wrong, for life is neither born nor does it die. Thus, what you call death is not your master, for you can never die. The eternal life I spoke of is not given as a gift of righteous living. Eternal life is a gift you give yourself by becoming what you are. In traveling this eternal journey, you must die daily if you are to live; for to die is to change. The young boy must die if a man is to be born. As the caterpillar's cocoon is torn open, the caterpillar is no more; instead, a butterfly is born. Such things you are quick to call change, but do you not see that they are a death? What you call death is actually the changing quality of life. To change is to die, but to change is to truly live.

When a loved one leaves you, it is because he knows that he must live. He casts aside the garment of his body and enters a quality of life that you have thus far deemed unnecessary. He has climbed the mountain and disappeared from your view in the shrouds of mist that surround the summit. He cannot tell you of his journey, for you must climb the mountain yourself.

If he wanted to speak to you, his message would be one that I taught when I was upon the Cross. Remember when I spoke to the thief upon the cross, and how I promised him that we would be together in paradise? Do you not realize that I was speaking to both men who hung beside me and to you as well? Do not be like the thief who would not listen. When you depart from the temple, you enter paradise. In paradise there is no pain, only wholeness. In paradise there is no condemnation, only understanding. You experience this wholeness as well as illumination. Your problems are not over, because they are a part of your soul. Instead, you see the dark places within your soul as opportunities to let your light shine, to grow in greater awareness of God. The problems are not tests given to you by your Father, but choices you made during your eternal journey. They are threats not to you, but to that part of you that must meet with oblivion — your ego. From this new summit of experience, you can see other peaks of understanding; thus, you can see your overcoming.

You may ask, "Is there more to paradise? What lies beyond? Is there a hell?" Yes, but only if you consider facing your ignorance hell. This path is steep, but it leads to a summit of human experience. "In my Father's house are many rooms." Some beings fall asleep and rest; others return to the Earth and take a new body. Still others have completed the necessity of earthly experience and move into realms you cannot comprehend.

In the midst of all these things there is a resurrection that awaits you; but you will not rise from a grave, for you are not your body. Instead, you will rise up from ignorance and into the eternal light of the morning Son. There will not be a day when I come and climb the mountain for you. Can you teach a child to walk by always holding his hand or holding him in your arms? Have you ever held a young child in your arms? After a time the child must move. He wants to walk. I love you, and thus I could not hold you so closely. Instead, I must walk behind you where I cannot be seen but only felt. When you stumble, stop, turn not around but within; and then the Christ will steady and guide you.

Remember, I am with you always. Each time you turn to the Christ within is a resurrection day for you. It is a day of celebration and new life. It is a time when you die to old patterns of thought and begin to live. When you observed my empty tomb, the old patterns of thought began to crumble. That day was as much a resurrection day for you as it was for me.

For you, death is a great unknown; but all change brings an unknown aspect of life. In truth it is change or death that brings life. If I had not died, I could not have risen. Without the Resurrection, my disciples would not have found the courage within *themselves to live as I had taught them. My death gave birth to Truth upon the Earth. At that moment, the seed of Truth was born in the souls of many. You need not fear death, for in Truth you can never die.*

A View of the Master's View

I remember years ago when I pondered death. One evening I was meditating on death and to my dismay no new insight came. I pondered why this might be. I soon realized that I was considering death to be life's opposite. The truth came slowly: life has no opposite. Death is a part of the journey of life. The fear of death rises because it is the least understood portion of the journey.

There was a time when I feared death, but now that time has passed. It is not that I understand death but that I do not fear change. That is what death really is. It is a change in the movement of life. Life does not cease when we die; it only changes. When change as a way of life is no longer feared, then death will lose its sting.

I have realized that life is not static; it is a dynamic, growing, evolving process. To realize this is to invite change. What lies beyond death I do not know, but I am sure there will be opportunities for growth.

There was a time of growth in my life when I

experienced the Father in a time of prayer and had
no conscious awareness of my body. The conquer-
ing of death continued as I realized that I am a
spiritual being who inhabits a vehicle of expression
called a body. There may come a time when I shed
the garment of the body that I now wear, but I will
not cease to be. The shedding of the garment will be
a change, but life is a change. To truly live is to be
consciously involved in an eternal process called
eternal life. To live eternally is to be continuously in
the process of change. Immortality is not a gift I
receive when I die. Life is a gift I accept when I
change daily. Perhaps that is what Paul meant when
he said that he died daily.

In pondering death, I tried desperately to relate
the experience of death to life and to my understanding of life. Early in my childhood I knew that I
was responsible for my life and that I would make
choices that would determine its direction. Many
people hold this belief about life, but many seem to
discard it when it comes to the stage of life called
death. They would tell me that when it comes to
death, I have no control. God will come and I will
leave my earthly body. Such a belief left me with
the feeling that life is without consistency. For a
time I carefully stored this false belief and the problems it caused in a corner of my mind. As life pro-
gressed, I knew people who seemed to be in charge

of their lives even to their last breath. I studied the life of the Master and marveled at how He made the choice to leave His body rather than accepting the often expressed idea that death is outside our control. Jesus, in uttering the words, *"Father, into thy hands I commit my spirit!"* said to me that death is a soul choice. We are masters of our lives even to the last breath. To be sure, many people do not make this choice consciously; nevertheless, it is a choice they make.

Death has lost its sting. I realize that I am in total control of my life even to the experience of death. I am not my body, for I am a spiritual being without beginning or end. Consequently I will never cease to be. Death is change, and all change leads to another opportunity to live.

The Master's View of . . .

The Last Day: Heaven and Hell

"Repent, for the kingdom of heaven is at hand." — Mt. 4:17.

"But I say to you that every one who is angry with his brother shall be liable to judgment; whoever insults his brother shall be liable to the council, and whoever says, 'You fool!' shall be liable to the hell of fire." — Mt. 5:22.

The Master's View

The Last Day: Heaven and Hell

There is a tree that must be destroyed. It is not enough to cut it down, for its roots lie deep in humanity's early beginnings. In the beginning, people observed the light and the darkness of each passing day. They feared the night, were paralyzed by this fear, and failed to realize that the night had no reality of its own. So dark was this shadow of ignorance that they failed to see that the night was simply the absence of light.

They next observed their own being and thought they could see two sides of their nature. One they called good and the other evil. It was from this faulty understanding that they assumed the Creator also has a light and dark side. They assumed the Creator could love and at the same time inflict pain. I ask, "Can the same stream give forth pure water but at the same time poison those who drink of it?"

The belief in the reality of a dark side of the Creator has cast a long shadow upon humanity's spiritual understanding. From this shadow grew the roots that nurtured the tree which bore the fruits called heaven and hell. As people harvested the tree, they felt that the good should be rewarded by eating the fruits of heaven and that the evil should be punished by eating the fruit called hell. In the light of the noonday sun, you will know that there are no good or evil persons. There are only those whose lights shine brightly or dimly. When I was with you, I spoke of heaven and hell. I used your terms; but you used your meanings. Your ears were not attuned to Spirit; thus, you heard what you wanted to hear. Now listen, and those who have ears will truly hear.

The time was drawing near for me to begin my ministry. I thought of how people were always searching for some distant place of peace and harmony. Sometimes they called it the kingdom of God; and sometimes they called it the kingdom of heaven. In beginning my public ministry, I wanted to convey the heart of my teaching; and I did. I proclaimed, "Repent, for the kingdom of heaven is at hand." I proclaimed this truth because I had found heaven. It is not a reward to receive after death, but it is a living reality. I alarmed many when I said, "Change your thinking, for the kingdom is now." You can have it now. Still, those who followed me looked for a sign and for the kingdom. I startled them when they learned that they, as individuals, must find the kingdom of heaven just as I did. I told them, "... The kingdom of God is in the midst of you."

I spent most of my ministry explaining what this kingdom was like so that, when it was discovered, it could be recognized. In parables I revealed its nature; and the wall which separated you from heaven began to crumble.

I said the kingdom was like a mustard seed. It begins small but grows until it is a great shrub. Plant this idea within you, and you will realize the growing quality of the kingdom of heaven.

I said the kingdom was like the yeast that leavens the flour. Eat of this bread, and you will know that heaven begins in a certain portion of your life and then spreads until it touches every fiber of your being.

I spoke again of the value of the kingdom. It is like the pearl of great price. It is so precious that you will sell all you have in order to obtain it. If you acquire the kingdom of God, you will know the richness of life.

Could such parables decribe a place? What is it that is priceless and at the same time grows? What is it that spreads all throughout your life and at the same time is something you have now? And remember, all this is within you. My friends, it is so simple. It is your growing awareness of God. What else could be more precious? Think of how your awareness of God grows and spreads until it touches all the areas of your life. This growing awareness of God is at the core of all the parables. It is the reward for everyone; it is what you have now; but it is also what you seek.

And what of hell? Is it the place the leaders of the church proclaim? Can you love your children and then blindly turn your back upon them and cast them forever from your presence? If you cannot do such a thing, how could your heavenly Father? Fear and punishment only cause you to turn away from God. Yet, it is not God you shun; it is the church. Still, there is a puzzle because I spoke of hell. You heard the word and assigned your own meaning. Listen now, and you will hear the Father moving deep within you and feel the stirring in your soul: Hell is not a place of suffering, but it is a state of purification.

Observe the order of the universe. You will know it is a spiritual universe governed by spiritual laws. Each law holds within it harmony or chaos. According to your use of the law, you determine whether your life is harmonious or whether it is chaotic. Each law is like a coin that has two sides. One side of the coin will buy you peace and pleasure, while the other side will purchase war and suffering. If you choose to suffer, you will sink into an abyss of despair.

As you sense the Father within you, the despair will be drowned by your desire to be free of your travail. It is this desire to no longer suffer that is the spark which lights the fires of purification. The spark is the light of Spirit within you.

When I spoke of hell, I often used the word Gehenna. Gehenna was a place where all the refuse of Jerusalem was cast. Eternal fires burned there to purify that which was discarded. Can you see why there is a hell fire burning within you? The purpose of the fire is to purify the erroneous beliefs that have caused the suffering in your life. This suffering is true travail because it gives birth to a new you, free of erroneous beliefs; thus, free of suffering.

However, the day will come when hell will be purified. You will no longer suffer, because you will use the coin of the realm to purchase only peace and harmony. You will no longer resist the inner stirring of the Father within you. You will begin to move forward in life when only nudged by the finger of Truth. The new birth is continuous now, and there is no suffering. The darkness of the soul is not purged by fire, but dissolves in the guiding light of Spirit.

Now the tree which bears the fruit of heaven and hell is no more. All that remains is to reveal the seed that fathered these two ideas. There is no place called heaven or hell; but you are not free of the judgment day. There is a last day. The last day is a time of the wrath not of the Father but of the laws of the universe. Every day of your life is a judgment day, because it is a day when you reap the harvest of your past thoughts, feelings, words, and deeds. It is the last day because now the harvest has come. Truly, the last day may seem like hell if the soil of your mind has nurtured seeds of negativity. Or the last day may seem like heaven if the soil of your mind has received seed from the land of harmony.

*The last day is not a time to be feared, but a day to
observe the fruits of your life. If the seeds have
fathered weakness, anxiety, illness, and poverty, then
plant a new crop; your next judgment day will bring
a harvest of strength, peace, wholeness, and abundance.*

A View of the Master's View

Have you ever thought that your beliefs reflect
your state of consciousness? Have you ever considered what your ideas of life say about you?
Heaven is that which all people seek; and truly,
there must be a heaven, or we would not seek it so
diligently. As I have discovered from my confronta-
tion with the Christ, the problem is where we seek
this state of harmony. Heaven is not a place, but a
growing awareness of God. What could give us total
peace and fulfillment but a greater awareness of
God? Regardless of our ideas about heaven, they
cause us no real problems, and they are a testimony
of the innate goodness within us. Such a belief says
that we are seekers of goodness.

It is the belief concerning hell that has always
troubled me. The dilemma occurs when we hear the
belief that the God who is Love may also turn away
from His children and cast them into a punishing,
burning hell. People will argue that we are not

God's children unless we obey His laws. Can such a belief contain any degree of even human logic, let alone spiritual logic? Either we are God's creation and thus, His children, or we are not.

Still, there were so many references to hell in the teachings of Jesus that I was disturbed, until I discovered that Jesus' hell was a state of purification. True, there was suffering associated with it; but the suffering was self-inflicted. In fact, it was the suffering that caused me to think that perhaps there was a better way to live. With this thought, the process of purification began; and I became a part of the spiritual process called hell. It seems strange to call hell a spiritual process; but what else could I call it when it was revealed as a period of growth? The fire that burns inflicts no pain; it only purifies.

Of course, with my new understanding of heaven and hell, my traditional view of judgment collapsed. As always, I was reminded of the idea that anything that is truly spiritual is eternal. If this is so, then what of this judgment day that lies in the future of all people? How could a day that is to occur in the future be spiritual? The answer was quite simple. It could not. However, once again it was apparent that the last day was a part of the ministry of Jesus. The call went out from within me for the answer; and the answer came. The judgment day must be every day to be eternal. It is called the last day because it is a day of reaping. The fields are heavy with the harvest. Our previous thoughts and feelings are manifesting in our lives. Some bring harmony and peace, while others bring anxiety and despair.

Lift up your eyes. Do not be sad, for today is a day not only of reaping but a day of sowing.

The Master's View of . . .

The Devil

"Begone, Satan! for it is written, 'You shall worship the Lord your God and him only shall you serve.' " —Mt. 4:10.

"You are of your father the devil, and your will is to do your father's desires. He was a murderer from the beginning, and has nothing to do with the truth, because there is no truth in him. When he lies, he speaks according to his own nature, for he is a liar and the father of lies." —John 8:44.

Do you have ears to hear? Listen to the words I spoke long ago of the devil: "He was a murderer from the beginning, and has nothing to do with the truth, because there is no truth in him. When he lies, he speaks according to his own nature, for he is a liar and the father of lies." *Do you see that the first lie ever uttered by satan was his own existence? Do you understand that I am saying there is no devil?*

During the time I walked the Earth, I could not openly proclaim this truth, for mankind was not prepared. Mankind was not ready to assume responsibility for his life and the world. But still the truth was there surrounded in the shrouds of mist for those with ears to hear: " . . . There is no truth in him."

Many will soon hear these words but not believe them. They will cry out, "No, this cannot be." One would think that the world would rejoice to know that the existence of satan was the greatest fraud ever perpetrated. People have been fooled by a mask made with their own hands.

What could be better than for mankind to know the truth that there is no evil force to oppose the will of the Father? When this truth is accepted, a search will begin for the origin of the woes of the world. The answer is etched upon the minds and hearts of all people. Human beings have supported an idea of an evil force or devil because of their inability to assume responsibility for their own lives.

Remember when I told my disciples, "I have yet many things to say to you, but you cannot bear them now"? The time has come for the shroud to be lifted and for the unbearable to be borne upon the shoulders of mankind.

You may stumble under the heavy load of responsibility if you are not fully aware of the nature of the devil. Shortly before I began my ministry, it is written that I was led into the wilderness where I fasted for forty days and forty nights. After this period of fasting, I was confronted with a part of my human nature called the devil. As I stood upon the threshold of my ministry, I achieved total dominion and mastery over my life. That aspect of people which confronts them with choices and encourages them to make decisions that do not enhance their own spiritual growth is called the devil.

As I was about to embark upon my mission, that part of me called the devil uttered these words within me: "If you are the Son of God, command these stones to become loaves of bread." Within that temptation is a choice that continuously confronts you: Use your spiritual capabilities for selfish purposes. The rational mind would argue, "I'm hungry; I haven't eaten for forty days." Have you ever rationalized an event in your life to fulfill some selfish purpose? You see, this choice is one we all must face.

Because I knew my Source, I answered, " ' . . . Man shall not live by bread alone, but by every word that proceeds from the mouth of God.' " *My nourishment was not bread but spiritual nourishment, spiritual ideas. Ideas are the mode of expression of the Father, and mankind is nourished by them. I vaulted the first temptation or choice one must face—using talents and spiritual faculties for selfish purposes.*

A second choice quickly followed. I was "taken" to Jerusalem and placed upon the pinnacle of the temple. There the devil spoke these words: "If you are the Son of God, throw yourself down; for it is written, 'He will give his angels charge of you,' and 'On their hands they will bear you up, lest you strike your foot against a stone.' " *I answered,* "Again it is written, 'You shall not tempt the Lord your God.' "

In my time, if a man were to jump from the pinnacle of the temple without injury, he would have been declared the Messiah, and the people would have rallied around him. My people would then have expected armed conflict with the occupying forces of Rome. I could not do so because my kingdom was not of this world.

In this temptation, that part of my human nature and yours has picked an intriguing guise. The choice is whether or not to use our talents and spiritual powers based upon the opinions of others. If I had jumped, it would have been what was expected.

However, I am the master of the unexpected.

The last and possibly the most appealing choice followed. Again, the devil took him to a very high mountain, and showed him all the kingdoms of the world and the glory of them; and he said to him, "All these I will give you, if you will fall down and worship me." *How appropriate were those words "fall down." If I were to worship that part of myself capable of producing negativity, it would have been a downfall of astronomical proportions. Yet the choice is an astronomical one that you face: should you use spiritual powers to bring yourself worldly praise and glory? I knew that glory belonged to the Father, so I replied,* "Begone, Satan! for it is written, 'You shall worship the Lord your God and him only shall you serve.' "

After my ascension, I returned and told my disciples of this occurrence in my life. It was necessary for them to know, for they would face the same temptations. Even you have been given stones to turn to bread. You have stood on the pinnacle of the temple and you have surveyed the kingdoms of the world from a mountain peak. Remember, you have been given dominion over your life. Even though you stand in the light of this awareness, know this of the devil: " . . . there is no truth in him." *Then you will hear these words:* "This is my beloved Son, with whom I am well pleased."

A View of the Master's View

For many years, I have not dared to speak what I felt to be true; but now I can. The devil is dead. There. I have said it. The confidence and depth of feeling behind these words are not as strong as they might be because I realize that to utter them is to accept responsibility for my life. It is to affirm that I am responsible for the negative conditions manifested in my life. Such an admission does not come easily.

There have been times when I thought I could feel the presence of an evil power. I was not prepared to accept the truth that these negative feelings were the result of erroneous beliefs I had been nourishing and harboring for years. The feelings were terrifying; thus, I declared them to be the work of the devil. It became so easy to blame all the chaotic happenings on the "father of lies." Little did I know that the devil would stand blameless before the courts as I declared my innocence and accused the evil one.

Now I know that no one is guiding me down a path of destruction. If I walk such a path, it is of my own choosing. This does not mean that the part of me that produces negativity and causes my downfall as a spiritual being is completely uprooted from my consciousness. It simply means that I am aware that this portion of my human nature must be up-rooted. With such an awareness, I stand ready to encounter the temptations of life.

I am aware of the possibility of using my talents for selfish purposes. I am aware of the possibility of governing my life based not upon the Spirit of truth that dwells within me but upon the opinions of other people. I am aware of the possibility of using my talents to bring worldly praise upon my lower self.

If I fall before these temptations, I have no one to blame but myself. You see, not only is the devil dead, but there is no devil. Satan is a tree without roots. He is a grape without a vine. Never again will I take fruit from that tree or drink of the wine of that grape. I accept my own responsibility; thus, I am truly free.

The Master's View of . . .

The Second Coming

"Lo, I have told you beforehand. So, if they say to you, 'Lo, he is in the wilderness,' do not go out; if they say, 'Lo, he is in the inner rooms,' do not believe it. For as the lightning comes from the east and shines as far as the west, so will be the coming of the Son of man."

—Mt. 24:25-27.

Have you ever been puzzled by what I said to you long ago? I said that I would come again, and for years many of you have eagerly awaited my arrival. In your waiting, you have raised your eyes so that they searched no longer in the Earth but in the skies above your head. Your waiting time has been a period of growth and anticipation, but you must know by now that I will not come in such a manner. You will not be able to proclaim, "Here He is; He is come again."

Intuitively, you know the reason why this is so. Instinctively, when you are in pain, you call my name; and many feel my presence. You call my name because you really know that I have never left you. It is as if my words are a part of your soul: " . . . Lo, I am with you always."

You will never be able to say of me "Lo here" or "Lo there" because in Truth, I have never left you. But still, I shall come a second time; and we will become one. I eagerly await our reunion. I will come to you when you cease searching the skies and begin to search your own soul. I will come not one more time but many. In fact, I have come many times already. You see, the second coming of the Christ is a personal experience. It happens not to a world but to individuals.

I can never enter your life as long as you fail to understand that the Christ must be born in you. That is the true significance of my second coming. Remember when I said that some men and women would come with me and that others would be left behind? I spoke, but only the illumined understood. The men and women I spoke of are positive and God-centered thoughts and feelings. The negative thoughts and feelings must be left behind to perish, for they have no place in the New Jerusalem of the second coming.

The wars and the rumors of war that I spoke of are beginning within you now because this truth is shattering your accepted beliefs. The earthquake that will shake your soul has already begun. The sun and moon are now darkened because your orderly universe is no more. This is the beginning; so rejoice. The time is near when I will "come again," and the Christ will be born again in you.

A View of the Master's View

One of the greatest enigmas I have encountered is the idea that Jesus will come again. I guess it is not so much that I am puzzled by His coming again as it is that I am puzzled by what He is to do when He arrives. For many, it should be a time of despair, judgment, and eternal punishment. But I can find no evidence that He would condemn. I am also disturbed by the idea that Jesus will come, solve our problems, and create a kingdom called the New Jerusalem upon this planet. It seems to me that while Jesus was here, He made it quite clear that His kingdom was not of this Earth. In fact, He declined the opportunity to establish such a kingdom. I ask you as I ask myself, "Who can solve our problems?" There have been times in the past when I wished that someone could solve my problems for me, but I have learned that I must accept responsibility for my life. I am a believer that with God all things are possible, but I have discovered "mission impossible" is living someone's life for him.

Remember how people proclaimed that Jesus had healed them? What was His answer? How many times did He say, "It is your faith that has made you well"? With that statement, Jesus was not denying that He had a role in the healing, but that ultimately it was not His faith but theirs that made them whole.

However, this does not mean that I am left solely to my own resources to solve the mysteries of my soul. This is why the second coming is so meaningful to me. The second coming is not an experience that all mankind shares simultaneously. The second coming is an individual happening that comes when a person is ready and receptive to such an experience. It begins when we know for the first time that the Christ is our own potential. Such a discovery will be no less fulfilling than the anticipated and long sought after literal second coming. In fact, it is not an experience of fear and waiting to see if one has been doomed or saved, but an instantaneous knowing that one is God's beloved child. It is the foundation upon which the New Jerusalem will rise.

The Master's View of . . .

Salvation

"For the Son of man came to seek and to save the lost." —Luke 19:10.

" . . . the Son of man came not to be served but to serve, and to give his life as a ransom for many."
—Mt. 20:28.

You are not lost, for the Father and I know where you are. To be truly lost, you must have forgotten your way and have no one to guide you. Lift up your eyes and be guided by the morning star that the Father has sent for you. The darkness is fading; the Spirit of Truth within you is like a brilliant beacon that beckons you into all Truth. You are not lost; you have simply lost sight of what you truly are. That is why I came. I have not come to save you, for who can save what is not lost? I walked the Earth and became the mirror of each person's soul. Just as the mirror reflects your true image, so I am a true reflection of what you are. The longing you have for me is your Christ Spirit seeking to be awakened in you. This longing is like the new song quivering within the heart of the composer, seeking to join the vibration and rhythm of the universe.

When you feel lost and cry out in your despair, it is the living water within you crying out to move and flow. It is as if the water is frozen or merely trickling through your veins. It is the illumination or knowing what you are that will thaw the living water and bring torrents of good into your life. It is not through my death that you live. It is through living your own life that you can overcome death. Do you not see that my blood was my life? Do you think that the blood I shed on the Cross can save you? It was the life I lived that can lead you to your own resurrection. The blood shed on the Cross was to be a symbol of my life, not my death. Do you not remember that when I celebrated the Passover with my disciples, each man drank separately from the cup? You too must drink from your own cup.

Our Father does not desire sacrifice. Such an idea arose in your mind because you knew of no other way to do the Father's will. It was through my life that you saw the Father's will; and now, equipped with this knowledge of the Father's will, you must travel the path I have walked. I have said that my life was a ransom for many. Remember that a ransom is a payment that brings release from bondage for something that is already yours. It is like the table that has been prepared for you by our Father since the beginning of the world. Our Father was well pleased when I sat with Him and ate of His fruits. The Father watches you and tugs at your heart when you feel lost and afraid. The Spirit of truth is continuously turning you toward the light. However, many times you have turned away. I came that you might see the fruits of walking in the light and learn the signs that mark the path of the infinite. The burning truth that frees the living water is this: Follow me, I wait for you.

A View of the Master's View

In my younger days, I recall being told of the loving heavenly Father who was always watching over me. Then there was the day when I was told that God is not only loving but that God is love. If you were like me, you sighed and gave thanks for such a loving Presence in the universe. For a while I felt secure and listened intently to every word concerning my loving heavenly Father. Then the problem occurred. The problem was disturbing, but I was even more dismayed because no one seemed to share my dilemma. The crisis occurred when I was informed that the same loving God who watched over me was not only protecting and nurturing me but was also outraged and finding fault with me. In fact, if I did certain "bad" things, He would turn His back upon me, declare me to be lost, and sentence me to be punished eternally. Although the punishment was frightening, the horror was that few people shared my awareness of the conflict between a loving God and one that would punish me eternally. To believe I could be lost was to place my hands over my inner eye and to push aside the logical operation of my mind. This I could not do; so for a time I lived with the frustration of not knowing the nature of my Creator. Although I had chosen the frustration, I felt sure that greater understanding would come.

When I became a father, the nagging belief in a punishing God was put to rest eternally. It will never be resurrected. My own relationship with my child assured me that I could never turn my back upon him regardless of what he had done. When the idea of a punishing God was dead, I pondered freely the nature and extent of God. I soon welcomed the pure realization that there is only God. Spirit is not only the Creator but the created. I wondered if I were not part of the universe. If so, how could God turn away from me? It would be to turn away from Himself. Still there were times when I felt lost, but I discovered that those were the times when I saw dimly. I was like a child being offered a gift but not knowing where to find it.

It became evident that the concepts of salvation and the possibility of being lost originate not in the heart of God but in the dark recesses of the soul. The beliefs tell us nothing of God; they reveal much about us. They indicate that we feel there are times when someone has committed a mistake for which he must be punished and that no mercy should be shown to him. They reveal that some people feel an exclusiveness and superiority to others who occupy this planet. I have discovered that many of our woes occur because we persist in comparing ourselves with each other instead of comparing our new selves with the old selves of yesterday. For me the inner comparison is the only one that can prove helpful. Herein lies the forward movement of the race. When we have erased the idea that punishment and revenge are valid, we will have taken a leap forward in resolving the conflict created by the belief that we can be eternally lost. When we face ourselves, make our comparisons with ourselves alone, and attempt to see the best in others, the question of salvation will die in our minds. Until then, I can only cling to the Truth that Spirit knows where I am, and therefore, I am not lost.

The Master's View of . . .

Love

" . . . You shall love your neighbor as yourself." —Mt. 22:39.

" . . . Love one another as I have loved you." —John 15:12.

Your kings demand much of you. Their commands echo endlessly in the valley of your soul. They ask of you what they will never do. Each charge is a burden, and you respond by pounding your farm implements into weapons so you might taste freedom and be nourished by life. I am a king, yet I have offered you only one commandment: " . . . Love one another as I have loved you." With those words I offered you life. I presented you not a taste of freedom but a banquet. Why have you not heeded my call? I did not speak the words in the wilderness where there were no ears to hear. My voice resounded in the public places. My decree is not a call to serve a man; it is a call to serve all men. It is an edict demanding that you live in freedom and pound your weapons into tokens of peace.

Why do you balk at my commandment? Is it that you feel you cannot love as I loved you? Would I bid you do what could not be done? I commanded you to love because I love you. To love is to live and to hate is to die. To form resentments is to select your grave site; to seek revenge is to scar the earth with your shovel as you dig your own grave. To hate is to lie in silent repose listening to the sounds of the living.

You are half alive because your love rises and sets as the sun. Its inconstancy is as certain as the seasons. You give the gift of love to those who love you; and to those who hate you, there is no gift. The love I give another does not depend upon him; it depends upon me. To love another is not to find him in agreement with you. It is not even to find the sacred Spirit within him. It is to feel the heartbeat of God within you, and to know that all hearts beat with the same rhythm. Loving is a decision you must make. I chose to love those who nailed me to a tree. I spoke words of love I thought they would understand: "Father, forgive them; for they know not what they do." On that day the soldiers and pharisees did not hear my message, but did you? In truth our Father did not need to forgive the instigators of my death, for He never stopped loving them. As I hung upon the Cross I could feel the Father loving me, and it comforted me. Yet I could also feel His love for those who placed me upon the Cross.

Aren't you relieved to know that the Father's love depends not upon you but upon His eternal, loving nature? Our Father's love seeks only to give itself away. Receiving His love is a choice you must make. For years you have sought the Father's forgiveness. Why do you seek what is not necessary? God need not forgive you, for He has always loved you. Forgiveness is required when there are hatred and resentment. There is neither hatred nor resentment in God. You must forgive yourself, and you will feel the eternal presence of love.

If you are to love as I love you, there must be a return to the commandment of old—"... Love your neighbor as yourself." This is not a plea or a humble request; it is a statement of Truth. Until you love yourself, you will be unable to genuinely love your neighbors. Instead, what you call love will be a bribe or plea for approval of another. Love cannot pass around you; it must pass through you. If a river is to journey to the sea, it must flow within its own banks. Your love must first flow within the banks of your own being. Only then will it weave itself into the sea of humanity. If you restrict the love of God for you, then the soil of your soul will become parched land. My friend, you must love yourself if you are to love at all. why would you not love what is most dear to the Father—you, His beloved child?

Begin each day with a declaration: This is a day of loving. *On one of these glorious days you will pass even beyond this noble pursuit. You see, as long as you must seek to love, you are capable of hating. One day you will not seek to be loving. Hate will no longer be a possibility for you. You will have journeyed from seeking love to being love. You will be the image of our Father. You will be love, and therefore, unable to hate.*

A View of the Master's View

" . . . *Love one another as I have loved you."* Why
have I not heeded the divine call? One cannot heed
what he will not hear. I have listened to love songs
written by those who have not learned to forgive. I
have eagerly read books written by those who think
love is an activity of the body rather than the heart.
I have been like the child sitting on the carpet trying
to catch sunbeams streaming into the dust-filled
room. I have reached for a treasure where it cannot
be found. Yet, in my feeble grasping, I have tried.

I have loved those who love me, but in so doing,
my love became as a reflection in a mirror. It lacked
the reality of divine love. My love was a bribe in
which I was asking another to fill my emptiness.
None can give me what I must give myself. I must
love myself, and then the love I give will require
nothing of the one I love. Just as each man has to
hold the cup to his lips, so I must nourish myself
with love poured from my own heart. In searching
my heart for this love, I will eventually find a
wellspring of love, whose depth is the universe,
whose height is the heavens, and whose width is
timeless.

Now I am a listener, a seeker in search of the
depth of the universe. Always there are the Master
and His commandment, " . . . *Love one another as I*

have loved you." Why did He have to utter such a commandment? More so, why did He have to live the truth of His words? On occasion I have seemingly been content with my dislike of another. "He does not love me; why must I love him?" I have questioned. There is no answer. Instead, there are the commandment and the example of the loving Christed one. But if an answer were given, it would resound within me for eternity: "He does not need your love, for God loves him; but you must love him to know the depth of your own being." Such a love seems impossible for me, but there is hope.

Hope beckons me into the future, but faith and knowing will lead me today. To begin I must know God is love. How can I say God loves me and hold the idea that the Father will turn His back upon me? Even in my feeble attempt to love, I turn my back upon no one. Surely, God who is love itself can only do what love does best — love. Just as water seeks its own level, so God is loving. But in Truth God is more than loving, for God cannot stop giving Himself away. This challenges all mankind. The love that God is enfolds us now, and we must open our hearts to feel and experience this love.

For years I thought to forgive was divine, but the Master's view has lifted me. To forgive is human; to love is divine. Hating makes forgiving inevitable, while loving means never having to forgive. God does not forgive me; God loves me, and I must forgive myself. As I release my ill feelings, I am healed and able to know the love that even now enfolds and indwells me. Forgiveness is a human disease that is cured and prevented by love. Still, forgiveness leads us to a greater state of wholeness.

It is a state of wholeness in which the murderer, the rapist, and the saint are equally enfolded in the love God is. There is only one difference: the saint knows and feels the love, while the murderer and rapist have chosen not to experience love; and in so doing, it is as if they have chosen not to breathe the air that fills their lungs. The murderer is not a murderer because of his place or condition of birth. It is not because he has chosen not to love his fellowman or God. It is because he has chosen not to love himself. To not love oneself is to struggle against the future by failing to accept the present. It is to be so busy trying to not be what we appear to be that we are unable to be what we truly are.

Together we have begged forgiveness from a greater power and felt betrayed. God has not betrayed us, for God can only love us. We have betrayed our higher selves. We are not unworthy of love. God loves us, and no matter what we do that divine love will never cease. Just as the light disappears when we choose to close our eyes, so love seems to turn to hate when we condemn ourselves.

Let us begin at the beginning by loving ourselves. We shall look at our embarrassed images in the mirror, smile, and extend our hands in friendship. In grasping our outstretched hands, the images of our divinity will begin to emerge from within us and be reflected in the mirrors of our souls. As we grasp those hands, the dams built by our feelings of resentment will crumble and release the love imprisoned within. On that day we will love so steadily that we will be what we have always been—love. We have been like the poem in wait of a poet— always a poem yet waiting for a mind and a pen to give it expression. We have been love in wait of a reason to love, and we have found that love does not need a reason.

The Concluding Revelation

"When the Spirit of truth comes, he will guide you into all the truth."
— John 16:13.

There is nothing new under the sun, but discovering what has always been is what adds a quality of freshness to life. A Recent Revelation has been such an experience to me. I have been puzzled; I have been challenged; and I have been renewed. I have received two precious gifts of Spirit that continuously abide with me. They are the mark left by the movement of Spirit. The gifts of abiding peace and joy were received within. But they cannot be housed within the soul, for they belong to the omnipresence of God. The challenges of daily living continue; but in the midst of this peace and joy, the challenges are viewed as opportunities to express more of the Christ potential that lies within all people.

It is my dream that the revelations continue, for I am a spiritual infant. Although I am an infant, I have made the important step of weaning myself from the religious leaders of the world. In their innocence they tried to hold me in their arms so I could not walk. I was not allowed to question the ideas of the church and was told that certain things had to be accepted. I was encouraged not to think and, therefore, to remain ignorant of my own spiritual nature.

Now I walk, although at times I consider it to be staggering. Life is more challenging when I ask my own questions, but the answers are more fulfilling. It is one of the paradoxes of life that each person must walk the path of spiritual growth alone while all indi-

viduals are traveling the same road. It is not that assistance is not given to another; it is that each must follow his inner Teacher. The time has passed when humankind will listen to the parroting of the literal ideas found in the sacred books of the ages.

The new age calls forth a new group of spiritual leaders who do not profess to have all the answers, but who do profess to know where the answers lie. Such leaders will be prophets of prophets, for they will speak of their own authority. They will understand the great truths taught by the Master and serve these truths to the people of the world. These ideas will nurture and sustain us in our search for the presence of God that is the universe. The pilgrimages to the far corners of the world will cease, because each one will begin the eternal journey to the city of God within. It is portrayed as a city because, when each one finds it, he will dwell there.

These new leaders will have a dream. In the dream, the churches that stand upon the street corners of the Earth will crumble. The symbols that have turned to idols will turn to dust. The war, poverty, famine, and illness that now plague humankind will be long forgotten and not even recorded in the history of the planet. The reason for such a world will be that we have discovered the divine potential within ourselves and cannot rest until we have expressed what we know to be the truth of being.

The church building will no longer be needed, for each one will be aware that he is the temple of the living God. We will learn the truth, live it, and because of our living, join the Master in proclaiming, "I am the truth."

Now only a few even dare to dream such a dream. The eyes are closed and the vision comes. The eyes are opened and the dream fades. The day is coming when all will dream such a dream, and when we open our eyes, the vision will not fade.

Unity Village, Missouri 64065

Printed U.S.A.

153-F-5003-15M-9-81